The Symphony of Nature

English Poems

Dr.A.Govindaraju, Ph.D.,

National Awardee

Published by

மின்கவி

படித்திடு ! படைத்திடு !!

BOOK DETAILS

Title	:	The Symphony of Nature
Author's Name	:	Dr.A.Govindaraju
Copyrights	:	© Author
Edition	:	I
ISBN	:	978-93-6274-136-3
Year	:	March 2025
Book Size	:	5.5 X 8.5
Publisher details	:	MIN E KAVI (மின்கவி)
		E-Development & Digital Publishing
		www.minekavi.com
		Phone : 9626227537
Pages	:	128

Foreword

(Prof. A.R. Kumaresan)

I'm proud to write this foreword for my teacher's book, 'The symphony of Nature' a collection of poems that reflect his wisdom, compassion, and creativity Dr.A.Govindaraju's poems are a testament to his ability to observe the world around him, to reflect on the human condition, and to express his thoughts and feelings in a way that is both personal and universal.

Dr.A.Govindaraju's poetry collection is a treasure trove of emotions, thoughts, and experiences. Through his poems, he takes us on a journey of self-discovery, love, loss, and the human condition. His poetry is a reflection of his own life experiences, observations, and values.

Dr.A.Govindaraju's poems are set against the backdrop of his own life experiences, including his relationships, his career as an educator, and his observations of the world around him. His poems are also influenced by his cultural heritage and his values of compassion, empathy, and kindness.

I have had the privilege of knowing Dr. A. Govindaraju as my teacher, and I can attest to his passion for teaching, his love of poetry, and his commitment to his values. His poems reflect his personality, his sense of humour, and his ability to connect with others.

As I read through Dr.A.Govindaraju's poems, I was struck by several key takeaways. In "Politician's Prayer," he writes, "O God, please keep me unpolluted / And let not my will get diluted!" These lines speak to the challenges of maintaining one's integrity in the face of power and temptation.

In "Ottawa River Bank," he celebrates the beauty of nature and the joy of simple pleasures. The lines "Birds stay back owing to the rains / Waters glittering while the sun shines!" evoke a sense of wonder and appreciation for the natural world.

In "Gently," Dr.A.Govindaraju explores the gentle aspects of life, writing, "Gently the breeze creeps up the flower! / Gently the bell rings on the tower!" These lines create a sense of peace and tranquillity.

In "An Elegy on Stephen Hawking's Demise," Dr.A.Govindaraju pays tribute to a remarkable individual who left an indelible mark on our understanding of the universe. The lines "A man of disability and nobility / Equivalent to all the men of ability!" speak to Hawking's remarkable achievements and his determination to pursue his passions despite the challenges he faced.

In "Tea Day," The poet celebrates the simple joys of life, writing, "A cup of nicely brewed tea / Makes our life so pretty!" These lines evoke a sense of warmth and comfort.

In "An Ideal Teacher," Dr.A.Govindaraju reflects on the qualities of a good teacher, writing, "An ideal teacher should / Not work mere for bread!" These lines speak to the importance of dedication and passion in teaching.

In "Anger," he explores the dangers of anger, writing, "You may note down the word anger / Yes it is one letter short of danger!" These lines create a sense of urgency and caution.

In "Motherless Dove," Dr.A.Govindaraju expresses his grief and loss, writing, "Which can give more pain? /

When we lose our beloved." These lines evoke a sense of sadness and longing.

In "My Heart Plays a Melancholic Tune," The Poet pays tribute to a remarkable individual who has passed away, writing, "An able and noble person to the core / Hard to believe that he is no more." These lines speak to the importance of remembering and honouring those who have come before us.

In "Nehru is the Conjuror," Dr.A.Govindaraju celebrates the leadership and vision of Jawaharlal Nehru, writing, "He goes in front / As a friend / Just a trick, no stick, / Millions follow him forever!" These lines evoke a sense of wonder and admiration.

In "The Plight of a Pensioner," He reflects on the challenges faced by pensioners, writing, "You can take away my ATM card, / Instead offer me à soothing word." These lines speak to the importance of empathy and compassion.

Finally, in "The Sweet Words," Dr.A.Govindaraju celebrates the power of kind and gentle words, writing, "Soar words will leave scars / Sweet words will bring cheers!" These lines evoke a sense of hope and optimism.

Throughout this collection, Dr.A.Govindaraju returns again and again to themes of love, compassion, and the importance of living a simple and authentic life. His poems are a reminder that, despite the challenges and complexities of the world around us, we have the power to choose how we live and how we treat others.

I highly recommend Dr.A.Govindaraju's poetry collection to anyone who loves poetry, who values wisdom and compassion, and who is interested in exploring the human condition. His poems are accessible, relatable, and thought-provoking, and they offer a unique perspective on the world around us. As you read through this collection, I encourage you to reflect on your own life experiences, appreciate the beauty of nature, and cultivate kindness and compassion in your own relationships.

Congratulations, Dr.A.Govindaraju, my beloved teacher, on this remarkable achievement! I am honoured to have had the opportunity to write this foreword for your book.

A.R. Kumaresan

Head [Retd]Department of English

Erode Arts and Science College,

Erode – 638009

Poems tinged with beautiful ideas

Dr.S.T. Gunasekar, Ph. D

Retired Principal

Karur.

....

Dr.A.Govindaraju is known for his splendid academic exposure and constructive thought process besides his broad outlook and panoramic vision of contemporary occurrences. He is a keen observer and tries always to document the happenings, in his own style, for the benefit of future generations.

His microscopic eyes catch and record everything that impacts and makes him happy and emotive. Greedily he transfers the same into the minds of his readers.

He is a prolific writer who has already authored many books in Tamil on travel, human resources, literature etc.

His novel attempt to reflect his thoughts in the form of English verses is really appreciable. His poems are very simple to understand but expressively tinged with beautiful ideas in an expressive way to an extent that the readers can easily grasp the content and travel with the poet in tandem. The topics of the poems that he has chosen tell us vividly that he is a nature lover and a true human being loaded with natural and spontaneous emotions. The rhyming pattern he applied in his poems is truly laudable.

The readers enjoy his verses! Many more laurels to the poet!

S.T.Gunasekar

Preface

In my view, English is a fascinating language. I had had interest in English poetry when my English professors introduced Robert Frost and William Wordsworth during my college studies. I started my teaching career as Kinder Garten Teacher and I wrote some rhymes for KG kids. That was my maiden attempt at writing poems.

I developed more interest in seeing some of my poems published in commemorative souvenirs. While I was serving as Principal of English Medium Schools I wrote too many poems to suit different occasions.

After retirement, at the age of seventy-three, I collected all those poems meticulously and sorted them out.

I hope that the readers read these poems and cherish them.

Dr.A.Govindaraju **World Poetry Day**

Camp: Dallas,USA **21/03/2025**

My sincere Thanks to

My student

Prof.A.R. Kumaresan,Head (Retd), Department of English, Erode Arts and Science College, Erode

My friend

Dr.S.T. Gunasekar, Ph.D, Retired Principal, Rani Meyyammai Matriculation School, Karur

Dedicated to

Mrs.Rajathi Teacher, presently a nonagenarian, who introduced the English alphabet to me way back in 1964 while I was studying in 4th standard.

CONTENTS

An Enchanting Evening

The setting sun made the sky glow
The breeze was hesitant to blow!
A cluster of birds was visibly sitting
On the trees as its leaves quitting!

Children playing on the pine needles
Mom fed her baby some noodles!
Men were moving hither and thither
Despite acute November cold weather!

I briskly walked mile after miles
Reciprocating to the beaming smiles!

Ottawa River bank

Each passing day brings me cheers
On seeing a beaming smile of dears!
Birds stay back owing to the rains
Waters glittering while the sun shines!
Walking happily on the Ottawa River bank
Seeing boats that steadily spank!
Butterflies briskly land on flowers
Enjoying the honey and flavours!

The cheerful morning

Ah! it's no doubt, a cheerful morn,
Just now the Sun was born!
Hill echoes the sound of the horn,
And white snow covers the lawn!
Skylark sings merrily a song
Comes with the church's ding dong
The breeze passes through buds!
They often shake their heads!

Gently

Gently the breeze creeps up the flower!
Gently the bell rings on the tower!
Gently the dog waves its tail!
Gently the baby crawls like a snail!
Gently the dew dries up on the rock!
Gently the hen goes near the cock!
Gently the snail moves its mile!
Gently I look at them with a smile!

Lovely thought of God!

I love wondrous nature
And its aesthetic feature!
Silver stars at night
And cold moonlight!
Golden Sun at morns
Just when it was born!
A cold and tender breeze
When comes through trees!
Rainy clouds like bushes
Busily when it rushes!
Children play with toys
And cuckoo's sweet voice!
Nature we have got
Lovely thought of God!

My walking experience

I walked through a less travelled road
Twisting, turning and not so broad
Laid along the lay of the land
By the side, sky-high pines so grand!
Where the chorus of frogs filled my ears
The gentle breeze chilled with cheers
A flock of Canadian geese winged past
And the maple leaves laden with frost!
It was quite visible in the smoky fog
A beaver crossed the road carrying a log
While cyclists pedalling in bands
Lovers walked clasping their hands!

The Jungle
(A cascade poem)

I made a trip with my uncle
We trailed deep into a jungle
I saw the foxes in their home.

We planned for a trekking
And we set off after cooking
I made a trip with my uncle

We crawled through trails
Like tiny tender snails
We trailed deep into a jungle

First, we saw a jumping deer
Felt the air filled with fear
I saw the foxes in their home.

Note:
Cascade poems are a new form of poetry invented by Udit Bhatia in 2007. Instead of using meter or rhyme scheme, cascade poems reuse each line of the first stanza as a refrain in the subsequent stanzas. Thus, creating a beautiful "cascading effect".

The maple hurst

I am an unsolicited guest
Trekking inside of the maple hurst!
The sun's rays enter through the trees
I feel the magic touch of the icy breeze!

Carefully carrying a nut in its mouth
A black squirrel jumps towards the south!
I spot a beautiful grey-haired rabbit
Involuntarily I click my cam, it's my habit!

Though it is considered as a jungle,
I don't think here I am lonely and single!

Note:
This is not an imaginary poem. The poet trekked in the dense wood near the Ottawa River in Canada and composed this poem on the spot.

The unlit sky

The little stars twinkle in the unlit sky
The black-winged clouds restlessly fly!
Many wonders are there in His estate!
Slipping slowly into a trans-like state!

His creations are really wise and noble
But to realize it, I am intellectually feeble!
I siphoned a little from the boundless energy
This always enhances my mind's synergy!

I find flowing in my heart the endless joy
And I feel rejuvenated as a young boy!

The Morning Walk

The sky is blue and has no cloud
The cuckoo's voice is not so loud
Being Sunday, there is no crowd
Walking happily, I am proud!

The eagle, as usual, flies ahead
Sailing its big wings widespread
The rising sun looks too bright
Its rays are emerging straight!

Continuously walking, I didn't sit
Thank God for keeping me fit!

Strolling along the Ottawa River

The summer is almost gone
And the unwanted fall falls upon!
As usual, I put on my shoes on
And set off for a walk in the dawn!
Keeping my hands in the pocket
Of the specially bought jacket!
Strolling along the Ottawa River
Using all my muscle power
Manoeuvring the cold breeze
As good as the Canadian geese!

The withered trees

Due to acute cold weather
Each leaf falls like a feather
When all the leaves wither
The tree stands as a mother!

When heavy snow throngs
The trees stand like monks!
Ready to bear wear and tear
Even in adversity without fear!

Of course after a very long gloom
All the trees will happily bloom!

Trekking on the hill

Trekking on the hill
Depends upon your will!
Take a little pain
Of course for the gain!
Walk up in the shine
Sometimes in the rain!
You 'll walk thru' streams
Occasionally with screams!
You 'll have to mingle
To understand the jungle!
Silence is the keyword
While you go up forward!
As you go to the mosque
You must leave your mask!
Why and how you'd ask
Before you take up a task!
Ups and downs on the hills
So also in our life, it tells!

Note:
This poem was composed on 11.11.1995 at Berijem, Kodaikanal.

Earth Anthem

It's a beautiful blue pearl
To be saved by one and all.
A God's gift, the cosmic ball
Play safely, no alternative at all.
Plant a sapling every B'Day
Save her thru' this simple way.
No to plastic be your style
It's time to walk an extra mile!

World Earth Day: April 22

When you trek into the forest

When you trek into the deep forest
I request all of you to be the fairest
From the forest, nothing you can take
You can take only the memory pack.

You are there to know the Nature's role
Lose your body, see through your soul
Use the only language, the silence
Forget not that you are under surveillance!

You should not behave too impish
Resolve, not to leave all the rubbish.

A worth living

Truly life is really worth living
It's not in taking but in giving
When we show concern for others
The mind becomes as soft as feathers!
A plant doesn't consume its grain
The sky doesn't consume its rain
Honey bees don't grab the honey
And their functions are so many
Their main aim is simply charity
But men only indulge in disparity!

Anger

You may note down the word anger
Yes, it is one letter short of danger!
It slowly eats up the mental pleasure
And shoots up the blood pressure!
It makes your sweet utterances toxic
At times you even behave foxic!
Anger hinders smooth sailing
Sometimes you are also wailing!
If you keep it with you all along
One day or another day it'll boomerang!

Note:
The word foxic is coined by the poet which means foxy ie deceitful in clever way

An ideal Teacher

An ideal teacher should
Not work merely for bread!
It'd be an art of dedication
For the cause of Education!
Teachers always should read
So that readily they can lead!
Let us all take an oath
To dedicate to this path!
We can educate even a fool
Ability should be our tool!
Soda bottle enthusiasm is not the need
A real enthusiasm we need indeed!

Love

The term I like very much,
    My heart feels its sweet touch!
You show, no you pour love,
    Like the lovely voice of a dove!
Give your heart to have a tent,
    Whatever may be the rent!

Nehru is the conjuror

He goes in front
As a friend
Just a trick, no stick,
Millions follow him forever!

How does he do it?
How does he do it?
I would like to know.

He writes a book
Now you look
Just a trick, no stick
The world go thru' forever!

How does he do it?
How does he do it?
I would like to know.

He rules for a while
With a smile
Just a trick, no stick
He makes us in a better shape!

How does he do it?
How does he do it?
I would like to know.

Obstacles to tear

O children my dears
Please lend your ears.
Please come over here
A few words to hear.
It is for you this year
To make you all cheer
Do not have a fear
When troubles come near.
Put yourself into gear
To shine in all sphere
Never burst into a tear
Obstacles are to tear!

Note:

Composed on 18.6.79 when the poet was serving in Nehru Vidyalaya Senior Secondary School, Coimbatore. 1979 was earmarked as international Year of the child.

Award winner

Chutti Award was won
By the little happy one!
It is none other than
The active Adheeran!*

His favourite is the gym
And remains ever trim!
Enjoys evening bath
In a very special wath!

Soon he would roam
Here and there at home!

*Adheeran is the grandson of the poet.

Be a Morning Lark

Be a Morning Lark
Burning of mid-night oil
See that it'd not spoil
Your physical health
As it is your wealth.
Are you a late-night owl?
It I'll down your energy level.
Better go early to bed
And also early to get.
So, be a morning lark
To feel your mind spark
Do even when hairs turn grey
The early bird catches the prey.

Note:
This poem was composed on 2.3.2009 as requested by the poet's younger daughter.

Behind the bar

We were put in behind the bar
You may ask surprisingly what for!
Of course for the noble cause
By the mass and for the mass!
We happily thronged into jail
As fast as the river Nile!
Alas! We're given aluminium plate
So black, it looked like a slate!
Served little that too salt less food
It was neither bad nor good!
Queue for even nature's call
Bathing chance was not for all!
It was the hell, we were given
But it looked for us as Heaven!
Many went away on bail,
But Periyar* did not avail!

Note:

This poem was composed on 28.9.1992 in Central Jail, Chennai while the poet was imprisoned for participation in Teachers agitation.

*Erode District formerly known as Periyar.

Father's Day Message

Children need a gentle hand
While they sincerely try to stand
Don't support them as a ladder
Rather guide them as leader
Instead of stacking a lot of wealth
Better keep an eye on their health.
As the Mummy is their yummy
The dad should remain chummy
When a child gives a keepsake
Respect it always with a true stake
Children arc the future seeds
Allow them to sprout to thcir needs.

Free Birds

The white caught all the birds
No one could wander in the woods!
They went on suffering in a cage
Yes, it was the darkest age!
O Rama, you relieved Sita
O Krishna, you helped in Githa!
Alas! Nobody showed sympathy
To relieve the birds in empathy!
O Mahatmaji! You made a fight
To relieve them from the White
At last, you opened the cage
And also the Golden Age!
Now skylarks sing with cheer
And wander freely without fear!
All the birds became free
And're living on a single tree!

(Composed on 2/ 10/ 1977 at Coimbatore)

Gone and ahead

2001-A year of fear
To the near and dear!
It is a clear mirror
Which shows utter terror!
It rolled faster and faster
Leaving Gujarat disaster!*
It was not a year of silence
Rather filled with violence!
2002-the forthcoming year
Filled with happiness and cheer!
Let us save our nature
To shape our future!

*Bhuj earthquake, occurred on 26 January at 08:46

Happy New Year

Happy New Year swiftly advents
Adding meaning to our deeds!
Past is past; let it slowly vanish
Present moment-it is to cherish!
Yummiest dishes we can taste

Never touch liquor; resolve to hate
Energise yourself as if going to Mars
Waive at once all your evil thoughts

Yes! Resolve to scale the new heights
Evolve a strategy and think bright
Awake; arise and achieve your goal
Redefine your path to play a vital role!

Note:
An acrostic in poetry is a series of lines in which the first letters when taken in order spell out a word or a phrase. In this poem HAPPY NEW YEAR is the phrase.

I love and play

I love, I play, I drink my wine,
In youth, brief, blithesome hours of life!
Alas! morning will bc over! then noon
And evening will come soon!
The mouth will say ‘goodbye’ to teeth,
And wrinkled skin to my youth!
I’ll think about my golden past,
The days once lost ever lost!
Now I feel my youth is priceless,
Why should I make it useless?

Not at all

Searching for food daily
And talking no good vainly
Suffering more in the heart
And doing others suffer a lot
Simply ageing with greying hair
And dying one day is unfair
Do you think that I will fall?
Like those clowns, not at all.

My little flower

O my little flower
I've become your lover
What a beautiful you are!
You are my twinkling star!
I can give you the world
It is spring, age of gold!
O my dear as you told
For your love, I hold!
When I see you my dear!
I feel myself so cheer!
When you are by my near
Your words are so sweet to hear!
O my dear flower!
Will you love me forever?

Stay Grounded

Sometimes you are extremely happy
Many a time you are equally unhappy
Don't swing between the extreme ends
Psychologists hate these unhealthy trends

Life is, as you think, not a seventh heaven
Occasionally it will be as hot as an oven
Treat alike both the brickbat and bouquet
Or you will miss your way and go astray!

Wise or otherwise be well-rounded
And always try to stay grounded!

Teachers Day
(Acrostic poem)

Teacher's job is to mould
Empowering children in many fold
Adding feathers and hence bold
Confronting the competitive world!
Hone their skills in every way
Enriching knowledge every day!
Rigour themselves like a mother
Sweat a lot before they wither!

Dedicated and devoted to the core
Acting like a beacon on the seashore
Yelling in joy when they achieve!

Note:

1.An acrostic in poetry is a series of lines in which the first letters when taken in order spell out a word or a phrase. In this poem TEACHERS DAY is the phrase.

2. This poem was composed by the poet on Teachers' Day while staying in Janpath Hotel in New Delhi on 5.9.2003. It was the occasion of conferment of his National Award by Dr APJ Abdul Kalam.

Tea Day

A cup of nicely brewed tea
Makes our life so pretty!
It cheers the evening hours
Especially for the young lovers!
Tea tells friends not to bother
Gives them a bond rather!
When it is served so hot
Truly enjoyed by a lot!
Now my stomach is empty
Let me enjoy my high tea!

Note:
December 15th is International Tea Day

The Biodome*

My daughter prepared some muffin
I enjoyed it as my evening tiffin
Decorated with a perfect topping
One after another I was taking!
Extremely tasty, I was wondering how
Because of the main ingredient, the love!
That's why the homely food is too good
A long time ago, one thing I understood
Heaven under the sun is our home
Rather I would call it, a real Biodome!

*Located in Montreal, Canada.

Celebrate your life

I am celebrating my wife
And thus celebrating my life
Life is not always to lament
Rather, enjoy each moment

Life is nothing but a God-given gift
We should not spoil it by indulging in the rift
Leading a simple life is filled with pleasure
Alas! Many of us are always under pressure

Hurdles will be there, let us boldly face
We can wipe out totally by giving a chase!

The day begins with sunshine

The day begins with sunshine
And ends with drizzling or rain
The day begins with a pain
And ends with a loss or gain
Using our super brain
We can’t make single grain
Knowing that life is uncertain
Wealth by any means we obtain
Though it is an ankle sprain
We go down with an energy drain!

Walk an extra mile

Fearlessly pursue the big things
For which you have to add wings
Aim always for globalized success
And maintain a dignified nexus
Make sure to walk an extra mile
With your ever-beaming smile
Be decisive and as well bolder
In adverse, I'm here to shoulder
Your success even if tiny no matter
I will celebrate taking it greater

Note:
The poet composed this poem for his daughters on the occasion of Father's Day (21.6.15)

The Ozone

At last, a breath of the fresh air
Is going to be the rarest of rare!
For the prevailing pollution
We don't have any solution!

We've depleted the ozone layer
But we defend it as a lawyer!
'Grow trees' remains as a chanting
Felling of trees is more than planting!

Unless we redefine our need
Earth will succumb to our greed.

The plight of a pensioner

Because I receive a pension
Occasionally I receive a mention!
Since I am the source of income
In my family, I am enjoying the welcome!

You can take away my ATM card,
Instead, offer me à soothing word.
Take away all my bank balance
Please give me emotional solace.

I need the touch of a healing hand
Until my last breath in this land!

Note:
The poet is a teacher pensioner.
(Oct 1: world pensioners day)

Education

Acquire this indestructible wealth,
Otherwise, you will become filth!
But easily you won't bc able to get
Yes! Sincerely you have to sweat!

Okay! Do sweat while you study
And your life will become steady!
Do you want to rule the world?
Or simply wish to become old!

Be bold, arise, awake and stop not
Striking the iron while it is hot!

Welcome song

We welcome you with cheer
For the sports meet of the year!
See to believe our children's skill
And their stamina and will
They 're powerful to break a hill
Do you 've doubts still?

Best rice in the best paddy
A sound mind in a sound body!
So we make their feature,
To suit for their future!
We welcome you with cheer,
For the sports meet of the year!

Note:

Composed in 1977 when the poet worked in Shree Nehru Vidyalaya senior secondary school, coimbatore.

The most sacred womanhood!

As a babbling **Baby**
The real jewel of the family,
As an energetic and young **Girl,**
As a responsible and mature **Lady,**
An intellectual friend and guide
In the role of a loving **Wife,**
With selfless love as a **Mother,**
A second mother as a **Mother-in-law,**
For all the grandchildren
As a fascinating **Grandma!**
Ah! What a wondrous creation!
Man is an integral part of a wo**man**
Let's celebrate heartily
The most sacred womanhood!

Library awareness

Let us read books to develop our intellect
Let the libraries become the place of worship
There is no need to have more prisons
In a nation where there is a library in every street
Those who ceased to breath became corpses
Who ceased to read books are living corpses?
Let us add meaning to our life
For which we have to rush up daily to libraries
Go through the Epic composed by Kamban
In which the Supreme Being becomes human being!
Go through the story of our Mahathma Gandhi
In which a human being becomes the Supreme Being!
Many hurdles will come in the way of honest
Finally, they will win their battle, no doubt
Books only teach all these values
Those books are stacked in libraries!

Note:
This is a translated version. Originally composed in Tamil by Mr.V. Vimalathithan, vice president, Readers' Forum, Central Library, Karur.

A MAGIC TOOL

Acquire this magic tool
Or you'll become a fool!
Easily you cannot get
Yes! You have to sweat!
Okay! Sweat in your teens
Of course by all means!
You want to rule the world
Or simply to become old!
Be bold, arisc and stop not
Strike the iron while it's hot!

Love where you live

Dear friend, you have to love
The place where you live
If it is Rome be a Roman

I hope that you say Amen
Follow all the rules, please
Or you will be out of place
Conform to all the etiquette
Otherwise, you'll have to quit

Learn the prevailing tongue
In praise, continue to sing!

Strawberry picking

We visited a lush green farm
Against the warning of the storm
Many rows of strawberry bush
Seen the fruits just by a push

We moved hither and thither
Picked fruits one after the other!
Ate them as greedily as a child
To stop it we miserably failed!

Fell some fruits; may be one or two
While collecting in a bowl too!
Finally met the Canadian farmer
And paid him just ten dollars!

The Money

When a fool is having money
It may cause a lot of funny
No meaning in having wealth
Not used properly, it is filth!

Truly speaking, money is power
But only in the hands of clever
Looking for easy money is bad
Landing in trouble you ‘ll be sad!

The quick money makes you prosper
But later it'll bring even disaster!

The plight of a girl

A beaming smile was playing on her lips
Making a swift movement on her hips
Hypnotized by the mellow of her voice
All the teenagers chose as their choice
When the boys posed a surreptitious look
Feeling blue, bowed her head seeing a book
Kept calm, when the people jokingly talking
But she felt hurt when the teens were stalking
Coyly looking, she focused on her goal
Accordingly, she preferred to play her role.

Pop your way to success

Aim and pop your way to success
Amidst ups and downs, the mixes
Even if you are in sixes and sevens
Just think of the seventh heavens

Unless you are prepared to sweat
In future, you won't enjoy sweet
As long as you are a guitar untuned
You will leave many stones unturned

Simply sitting, eating and sleeping is a sin
Only a hard-working guy knows how to win!

Am I right?

It was the darkest night
No moon or stars at the height
Someone lit a small lamp
Hence I walked through a ramp

It spread a light of hope
As if I could win the globe
Should we curse the dark?
Light a candle; leave a spark

You can exhibit your might
Please tell me, am I right?

The Friendship

When you think you ‘re superior
You push me to feel inferior
We should feel equal, indeed
Irrespective of caste or creed

I don’t want to be a leader
Or you don’t need to be a follower
Let us walk together side by side
Keep all the other factors behind

There is no need to compare
But now and then, we have to repair!

A man of word not in deed

A man of word not in deed
Truly he is an unwanted weed
When the weeds begin to grow
All other crops grow very slow
The man who has no etiquettes
And has no very basic ethics
He becomes use less
Or totally useless
What is being a dead weight?
It's my view whether I am right!

Look at the food you eat

Before eating, say it is great
Look at the water, know it's worth
Without it you can't live on this earth
Look at your bike before you start
Think and thank part by part
Look at your vegetable vendor
Say: How are you? He would wonder!
Look at everything gracefully
Think of them very gratefully.

The noteworthy treasure

The sacred Thirukural couplets
Are nothing but Ambrosia droplets
It helps us to eradicate our vice
And shows ways to become wise
Thirukural is the most secular
That is why it is very popular
It is more than two millennia old
And a common one for the world
It is no doubt a noteworthy treasure
One can read and cherish at leisure!

An Ode to Bharathiyar

Bharathiyar is our renowned National Poet
As a valiant soldier, he fought against White
He was arrested and put in jail
But he never opted to come out on bail
He unfortunately died very young
But contributed a lot to the mother tongue
He talked about the women's liberation
And raised his voice for their emancipation
Though he lived in utter poverty
He always kept his respect and dignity.
Getting freedom was his only mission
For which he had forethought and vision!

An Ode to Dr.A.P.J. Abdul Kalam

No doubt, because of your zeal and attitude
You rose to this unimaginable altitude
In Rameswaram you were a little blossom
Now you are the first citizen! Awesome!
Due to your stability, ability and nobility
You have become a renowned celebrity
You are the only source of inspiration
To all the Indian youth having aspiration
Sir, today I am taking an oath
To carefully follow your path!

Note:

The poet handed over this poem to Dr. Kalam when he met him in Rashtrabathi Bhavan, New Delhi on 5/9/2003. Dr.Kalam had a glance through it with a beaming smile!

An Ode to Dr.C. Sylendra Babu

Honest and upright to the core
And hence I adorn him with lore!
He is courteous for righteous
But audacious against atrocious!
A nightmare to the gangsters
But a role model for youngsters
Always he looks like a young chap
He has many feathers on his cap!
Cycling is his high passion
He pedals across the Nation!

Note:
The poet is a close friend of Dr.C.Sylendra Babu, IPS. He has translated two of his English books into Tamil.

OKT is the best teacher (Acrostic poem)

O! You are the best teacher
Kindness is your fine fcature!
Teaching ability is your nature
Headmaster with a good posture!
Incredibly you 're doing wonders
You excuse even Himalayan blunders!
Always you 're busy like a bee
Giving a helping hand whether he or she!
Achieved fame in your life
Really nothing to children and wife!
Alma mater for you is the only matter
Just a reality! I don't flatter!
Await another feather to your cap
National award after a little gap!

Note:
Composed when Mr.O.K.Thiagarajan, Headmaster, DJHSS, Gobi was adorned with State Award in 1991

The smartest Teacher

I see the smartest Teacher
No words to sum up his feature
Today he gets down from his chair
And my heart gets a fracture
He is more than a preacher
Done much for this poor creature
I recall his golden past
Daily I recall him at any cost
The Bible says Jesus followed a star
Practically, I am following you, Sir.

Note:
written this poem when Mr.O.K.Thiyagarajan, HM, DJHSS retired on 31/5/1993

Teachers Day greetings

I take this juncture
To recognise your venture!
Your wholehearted dedication
For man-making education!
You're physically growing old
But mentally growing bold!
"Be brave" – once you told
I will show that to this world!

Note:
Teachers day greetings sent to Prof.R.Krishnamurthy, my English professor on 5.9.1984

Poem on Aruldoss

An uncompromising personality
Widely known for his integrity!
Praised often for his ability
Revered much for his nobility
With his dedicated sincerity
He exhibited his proven honesty!
While many turned as mercenary
He has been a perfect missionary!
When we rushed for his sympathy
We enjoyed thoroughly his empathy!
He is not only a good narrator
But also a bilingual orator!
I would like to make an application
To the Almighty with my supplication!
May God bless this disciplinarian
To live as a healthy centenarian!

Note:
Composed when the Gobi DEO Rev. S. A. Aruldass retired from his service.

Stupendous success

It's a memorable occasion
While relatives are on vacation
No iota of any commotions
Rather filled with emotions!
A time for laughing moments
And some musical movements
It's so informal and casual
In my view, quite unusual!
It's a stupendous success
Showcasing the loving nexus!

Note:
Composed on the 60th B'Day celebrations of my good friend Mr. Muruganand, Canada

A Great Teacher

You're a great Teacher
Very polite and pious in nature!
Rarely seen a person like you
Visionaries like you, are very few!
Reaching and teaching-your mode
Very well you deserve our ode!
Retired but energetic and young
Vibrant enough to spread your wings!
Reap many more winnings
Vigorously in the second innings!

Note:

Composed when my colleague Mr.R. Venkatraman, Physics PG Teacher, TNPL School, retired from service

Murali the Great
(Acrostic poem)

Murali the jack of all trades
Unanimously accepted by all grades
Resigned and gone- we don't believe
Always with us, he can't leave
Leader in the true sense
Innovative inquisitive and hence

Treating the children as his own's
Hearts in thousands he owns
Elevated to greater height

Guiding them as a beacon light
Really a loss –so our tears
Employed well – so our cheers
All we accord our best wish
The great Murali we miss!

Wish you Happy Birth Day!

It's the great Day of Birth
The day of landing on earth!
Carved yourself all the years
Shifting carefully into gears!
Adding value to your life
By taking care of your wife!
You're right in the right way
Wishing you a Happy Birth Day!

Note:
Composed to wish my son-in-law on his birth day.

Ding dong ding dong bell

Ding dong ding dong bell
Rohan went to near a well
Was playing with Daddy's cell
Into the well, suddenly it fell!
Alas! That made him very sad
And afraid much of his Dad
Mummy said he was mad
He too felt that he was bad
Dad said to him that's okay
Rohan laughed kay kay kay!

Note:
Composed to wish the little child Rohan on his birth day.

On seeing my grandson

I smiled through my pains
Felt a new energy in my veins!
Tears welled from my eyes
Seeing the little boy; a rare spice!

He charmed me with a power
Which I ever experienced? Never!
Sitting down in a stroller
Unmindful of this caller!

I think he must be a rare breed
Keeping no insignia of the creed!

Note:
Composed when I saw my newly born grandson in Canada.

Made for each other

Supritha the gem of women
Sriram the gem of all the men
Synchronizing in the wedding
And a new family is budding!

Both are made for each other
And hence mad for each other!
The dreams that they nurture
Would come true in the future!

Note:
Composed to greet Sriram and Supritha during their wedding on 11.7.2019 Kolar Gold Field.

A vibrant new family member

A vibrant new family member
To rule the world, remember!
Crying for milk, it's basic
And for sleeping, it's music!
Kayilan is his sweet name
I think it's a synonym for fame!
He has brought cheers
To all the near and dears!

Note:
written when the poet's second grandson was born in Canada.

An eye-opener

Your address was an eye-opener,
My colleague said," A brain sharpener"
We 're ruminating about your lecture
A beautifully depicted picture!

We 've to revamp the full structure
How boldly spoken at this juncture!
First, let us accept the degeneration
Then only we can think of regeneration!

You've brought the varsity into a shape
Which 'll find a place in the global map!
You 've added more feathers to its cap
And you 've sweated to keep it atop!
With your highly elevated thoughts

You 've motivated our taughts!
I'm sure they 'll bring laurels and ranks
So, kindly accept our sincere thanks!

Note:
Thanking note sent to Mr. Ponnavaiko, then vice-chancellor of Bharadhidasan University for his key note address delivered during the annual day of TNPL School.

Dog versus God

I wonder seeing its unwavering devotion
Not worrying about promotion or demotion
Patiently longing for the touch of empathy
from the people who never show sympathy!

The dog's silent and expressive gaze
is not understood by the human race!
Its loyalty and unconditioned love
Let us accept, truly we don't lurve!

For you, it may be a stray DOG
For me, it is another form of GOD!

Points to ponder

In life, avoid maintaining rigidity
Better to maintain elasticity
Expecting cent percent perfection
Leads to utter frustration!

In life, don't count the cursing
Better to count the blessings
Develop a feeling of positivity
Avoid the feeling of negativity!

In life, luxury is not at all necessary
That will lead to endless misery!

React or Respond

Well! You are physically well
But you are psychologically ill
Making the whole world a hell
May be one thing I want to tell

Don't allow your mind to rule you
Make it a good servant for you
People always react to a situation
Very few respond, it's my speculation

React means you are emotionally ill
Respond means you are emotionally well!

Basking in the sun

Children were basking in the sun
Happily making merry and fun
Happiness bubbled up in mingling
Coins in their trouser were jingling!

Many times they were wooing
Sometimes they were booing
They went to a nearby ground
And walked round and round

Aimlessly, they wanted to roam
Before they arrive at their home!

A beautiful flower

My lover is also a beautiful flower
O Butterfly, show her your colour!
O breeze, blow gently on my dear
So as to bring happiness and cheer!

She didn't commit anything wrong
O cuckoo, for her please sing a song
My lover is very sweet and funny
O honey bees bring some honey!

In order to enhance her romance
O peacock, now you may dance!

The sweet words

Soar words will leave scars
Sweet words will bring cheers!
When thoughts become weeds
That will lead to unethical deeds!

Words are the outcome of thought
Mending the thoughts is an art!
For which we have to read a lot
The Thirukkural, a treasure we got

Consciously we have to speak
Let the sweet words adorn our speech!

Doctor's Prayer

While I handle the surgical tool
Keep me focused, composed, and cool
I am not interested in collecting more fees
Rather, I will be happy with content and peace

After carefully dressing the wound what I feel
Neither my skill nor my drug, you would heal
I never asked you to keep me wealthy
To serve all, please keep me hale and healthy

Always guide me to engage in the right gear
And let me do my job with a moral fear!

Politician's Prayer

I heartily wanted to live better
Unknowingly jumped into this gutter
O God, please keep me unpolluted
And let not my will get diluted!

Never make me a greedy
Give me the energy to serve the needy
I'm not interested in the law of the jungle
Please let me live simple and humble!

I have a good agenda, and tasks are many
Please, don't make me run after money!

Teacher's prayer

I don't want simply to preach
O God! Give me the power to teach
Make me please, behave cordial
Even when the situation is an ordeal
Help me to be a devoted teacher
Otherwise, I will be branded as a cheater
Empower me to impart Ethics
Which are found plenty in our Epics
It's my duty to teach the lesson
Give me the power also to listen!

If you can

If you can again give it a try
Otherwise, continue to cry
If you can rise to win
Or you will be put in the bin
If you can resolve to work
You are not a lazy folk
If you can aim high
You are the smart guy
If you can have a dream
Do whatever you deem!

Wealth versus Health

Always you're running after wealth
Sometimes even ignoring your health
Try not to grab it rather from the filth
Apply your sense, necessarily the sixth
You don't have time to talk to your wife
And used to walking ever on a knife
You have to groom yourself to live life
Otherwise, you will be called a type
O my friend, please mind your mind
Stop, and allot some time to unwind!

Every situation has a lesson

If you are willing to listen
Every situation has a lesson
Even when the situations besiege
There will be a home- taking message
But many of us do not deserve
Because we hesitate to observe
When the wise people say something
Our mind instantly says it's nothing
We never accept due to the mind shut
Are we ready to change our mindset?

Emotional Balance

Are you an advocate of positivity?
Equally good, even the negativity
Laughing is not always good
Weeping is not always bad
Laugh while you laugh
Weep while you weep
Much needed is the emotional balance
Of course, it is a little bit challenge
Accept the people you meet as they are
Or you will indulge in emotional war.

Tonight will be dum dam (Acrostic poem)

Big flower pot is bright
Orange, red and white
New sparklers' delight

Funny! Am I right?
I readily grab this chance
Rockets ready to launch
Elite fireworks go high

Now and then I buy
In fact, they are fun
Ground spinners run
Highlight is Laxmi bomb
Tonight will be dum daam!

Note:
Composed on 11/11/2023, the Deepawali night.

A win-win attitude

Life has room for a better future
Don't fear changes think of its nature
If one door is getting closed
Another door will be opened
Look at your days ahead positive
Think seriously same alternative
Develop a win-win attitude
That will upgrade your altitude
A baby step is the basis for galloping
Of course, it will be challenging!

Shine like stars

The sun and the moon and the stars
They don't compete with any other source
Simply they shine and continue to shine
If you follow them that would be fine
When you compete you have to win or lose
Either as you wish you cannot choose
Try to optimise your skills in your field
Never bother much about the yield
Keep going, do your duty, that's all
One day you will reach your goal!

A B C D of Corona

Avoid hereafter giving a handshake
Better indulge often in hand wash
Coughing etiquette is a must
Distancing one metre is always best.

Eating nutritiously builds immunity
Fighting against Corona exhibit unity
Go out not- that should be resolution
Home staying seems the right solution

If there is a will there is a way
Join the war to keep the virus away!

Say cheers!

Many people cover their face with a mask
Knowing their hidden agenda is a big task
They smile; hardly have we known it is fake
Alas! Acting skilfully only for their sake!

Take it from me, always see eye to eye
That will make you feel high
When you speak, let it be heart-to-heart
Then you feel pain when you part!

No meaning in living for too many years
Have you ever said heartily, cheers!

O Corona!

O Corona! You 're omnipresent
Slowly becoming omnipotent!
You make everyone handicapped
And everybody is house-trapped!

Since you have begun to ransack
We have even avoided handshake!
Are you merciless? You spare no one
Without our consent, you drop in!

Sooner or later your wings will be cut
By the scientists' tireless effort!

Strongly we believe!

You have crowned yourself
And we have crippled ourselves!
You have given all a rupture
Yet we're unable to pass stricture!

You are too busy and even crazy
And making all of us dull and lazy!
You follow us stealthily like a stalker
Soon we will put you in a locker!

Enough we suffered; please relieve
Victory is ours, strongly we believe!

It's for a good cause!

Whether it is a village or a town
Feels the pinches of lockdown!
Of course, there may be some loss
But undoubtedly it's for a good cause!

The corona invades the entire world
Invariably it pounces on young and old!
What mankind sown in the past
Now reaps the consequences at last!

Having done all the anti-nature action
Facing an equal and opposite reaction!

We will overcome this crisis

People sit at home miles apart
Silently suffer and extend support!
The corona remains a puzzle
And emerges as a worldwide hassle!

It's high time to make a resolution
To keep ourselves more in isolation.
We 've to maintain our personal hygiene
Let it enter and embed in our gene!

We will overcome this crisis soon
Yes, probably by the end of June.

The talk of the town

The world is now under your possession
And hence there is an economic recession!
You*, the invisible ill equipped warriors
Travel smashing almost all the barriers!

You've already broken all the notions
Of the so-called super power nations!
Simply they raise sadly their eyebrows
And rush to hospitals in lengthy rows!

For the deceased silently we mourn
While you are the talk of the town!

*Corona virus

The Quarantine

Since I have been confined
I do feel somewhat refined!
None grabs my precious time
Wasting one's time is a crime!

The window pane is very wide
Rain or shine it doesn't hide!
No one can indeed ask
Whether I lowered the mask!

My companions are the books
And I help my wife while she cooks!

Note:
The poet was quarantined for fourteen days from 3/8/20 to 17/8/20 in Ottawa, the capital city of Canada

The quarantine effect

I was sitting quietly for hours
Like a crane on the bank of rivers!
As idle as a painted train
Rushing through a painted terrain!

Remained neither cheered nor bored
Truly neither disappointed nor lured!
Loneliness may weaken a person
Immensely felt when I was in prison! *

Here it was done away with reading
Yet some restlessness was invading!

Note:
*The poet was arrested and jailed for 14 days in 1993 for having participated in Teachers' agitation

O Corona! Quit India

Quit India as early as possible
Universally you're not plausible!
Intolerably you have become a nuisance
Tactfully you conceal your presence!

It's high time for you to move away
Never come back! Keep us at bay!
Disappear, please! You are taxing
India will invent soon a vaccine
And shall stop your undue taxing!

Note:
An acrostic in poetry is a series of lines in which the first letters when taken in order spell out a word or a phrase. In this poem QUIT INDIA is the phrase.

A B C D of life

Always Be Courteous.
Do Exercise and Feel Good Health.
Initiate and Just Keep Learning.
Maintain Non-violence Only.
Pray Quietly.
Respect Senior citizens and Teachers.
Maintain Values. Wear a mask
and Xpress Your Zeal to fight COVID19.

Note:
This is a free verse.

New year message
(Free verse)

Let us take an oath to maintain unity
even in diversity and adversity
by eliminating animosity and atrocity.
Equanimity and propinquity
are to be nurtured among
the multiplicity of people.
Let charity continue
but not for publicity
and cheap popularity.
Let the New Year foster affinity
and adaptability.
And let it bring forth the opportunity
to suit our personality,
nobility, ability and potentiality.

Stay safe on Escalators
(Free verse)

No distractions! Put away your mobile.
Confirm the directions of moving steps.
Take extra care when you step on and step off.
Don't let the shoe laces untied.
Grasp the handrail.
Stand in the middle of the step and face forward.
Hold children firmly by the hand.
Keep your clothing clear of moving parts.
Never put items on the steps or handrails.
Don't daydream or gaze about while riding.

One two three

One two three
An old apple tree!
Four five six
Ladder to fix!
Seven eight nine
Idea is fine!
Ten eleven twelve
Collect in a bowl!

Note:
composed for KG Children while the poet served as KG Teacher in Coimbatore way back in 1977.

I will shoot

This is my pen
Shines in the sun
O my dear hen
Shall I give you a bun?
This is my gun
I will shoot you for fun!

Note:
Composed for KG Children while the poet served as KG Teacher in Coimbatore way back in 1977.

My name is Paul

I am very tall!
To catch my ball
Ran along the hall
Banged on the wall
Made me fall
No injury at all
But caught my ball!

Note:

Composed for KG Children while the poet served as KG Teacher in Coimbatore way back in 1977.

O my cat

O my cat
Catch one rat
What you ate
Why do you hate?
Don't be late
To become very fat!

Note:
Composed for KG Children while the poet served as KG Teacher in Coimbatore way back in 1977.

Motherless dove

Which can give more rain?
It is only a dark cloud.
Which can cause more pain?
When we lose our beloved.
Who can shower selfless love?
The known God is our mother.
Alas! Now I am a motherless dove
That too without feathers!

Note:
-Composed when the poet's mother demised on 27.5.77

He was knowledge of the ocean

He was knowledge of the ocean
In the school a major portion!
Alas! He is gone out of station
Of course, in the very long vacation!
It's really an irreparable loss
For all, a beloved one he was!
Many hearts 're broken into piece
May his soul rest in eternal peace.

Note:
This elegy was composed when my colleague Mr.Karupiah, the English PG Teacher of DJHSS demised.

The torch bearer

The torch bearer who led the Nation
With a clear mission and passion!
Alas! The legendary figure is no more
When shall we hear the lion's roar?

The Golden Quadrangle Road scheme
Was his brainchild and dream!
And he made it possible very soon
For the millions it became a boon!

Not only a poet but also a statesman
Proved himself an all-round batsman!
His name will be carved in golden letter
In the history that will ever glitter!

Note:
An elegy composed on demise of Atal Bihari Vajpayee,the formerly Prime Minister of India.

An Elegy on Stephen Hawking's demise

Truly, a versatile genius is no more
Alas! Whose soul at last left the door!
Men may go and men may come
But he has left an intellectual vacuum!
A man of disability and nobility
Equivalent to all the men of ability!
Researched sitting in his wheelchair
Explored the entire enveloped Nature!
A life filled with lightning and thunders
Yet, he did many Himalayan wonders!
Amidst liars, fears, tears and cheers
He survived for seventy-six years!
Let his soul rest in ever-eternal peace
In his memory, let's plant some trees.

Note:

Composed when the great scientist Stephen Hawking demised on 14/3/2018

My heart plays a melancholic tune

The end has come for him so soon
My heart plays a melancholic tune
An able and noble person to the core
Hard to believe that he is no more
He was guiding like a beacon light
Keeping every fellowman in delight
He set his goals always atop
Alas! His story ends with a full stop.
Efficiently he did all the best
In eternal peace, May his soul rest.

Note:
Mr.R. Seenivasan, President, TNPL School Society passed away on 9.1.2024.

About the Author

Name: Dr.A.Govindaraju /Pen name: Inian
DOB: 08/03/1952 / Nationality: Indian

Educational Background:

B.Sc(Phy)., B.L.I.S., M.A(Tamil)., M.Sc (App.Psych)., M.Ed., M.Phil., Ph.D., Dip.in Gandhian Thoughts., Dip.in Teaching of English.

Published works:

- Published articles in Dinamani,
- Two research books, Two travelogues,
- Two translated books, Ten other books.

Work Experience:

20 years of teaching experience and 20 years of administrative experience as Headmaster and Principal.

Hobby:

Reading, writing, trekking, travelling, tree plantation

Awards:

- Justice S. Mohan Literary Award,
- National Best Teacher Award conferred by **Dr.A.P.J.Abdul Kalam**

Social media:

- **Face book:** Inian Govindaraju
- **Blog:** iniangovindaraju.blogspot.in
- **YouTube:** Dr.A.Govindaraju

Contact:

Email: agrphd52@gmail.com
Mob: +91 9443019884

www.ingramcontent.com/pod-product-compliance
Lightning Source LLC
Chambersburg PA
CBHW062141160726
48282CB00027B/901
* 9 7 8 9 3 6 2 7 4 1 3 6 3 *